THIS BLOOMSBURY BOOK

BELONGS TO

....

?HJ

.gov.uk

Fig. 1 Firefly

Fig. 4 Yellow Beetle with Black Spots

Fig. 2 Southern Green Stink Bug

Fig. 3 Red and Black Beetle

Fig. 5 Winged Desert Termite

Fig. 6 Bumblebee

Fig. 9 Sweet Potato Weevil

Fig. 7 Bush Katydid

Fig. 8 Slug Moth Caterpillar

Fig. 10 Woolly Caterpillar

*For my dad, Byron, who
allowed me to be a sleepyhead
and whatever else I wanted to be*
—E.P.

For Olaf, our entomologist
—D.S.

First published in Great Britain in 2005 by Bloomsbury Publishing Plc
36 Soho Square, London, W1D 3QY
This paperback edition first published in 2006

A CIP catalogue record of this book is available from the British Library

ISBN 0 7475 7602 5

Printed in Singapore by Tien Wah Press

10 9 8 7 6 5 4 3 2 1

All papers used by Bloomsbury Publishing are natural,
recyclable products made from wood grown in well-managed forests.
The manufacturing processes conform to the environmental regulations of the country of origin.

Ten Little Sleepyheads

by Elizabeth Provost · illustrated by Donald Saaf

BLOOMSBURY
CHILDREN'S
BOOKS

10

Ten little sleepyheads
talking to their toys.

One falls asleep
in the middle of the noise.

9

Nine little sleepyheads
reaching for a snack.

One falls asleep
on a crumbly cracker stack.

Eight little sleepyheads
giggling in a pile.

One falls asleep
with a dreamy little smile.

7

Seven little sleepyheads
playing peek-a-boo.

One falls asleep,
but we're never telling who.

Six little sleepyheads
crawling on the rug.

One falls asleep
nose-to-nose with sister bug.

5

Five little sleepyheads
begging for a book.

One falls asleep
as she tries to take a look.

Four little sleepyheads
toasty in their towels.

One falls asleep
while her baby brother howls.

3

Three little sleepyheads
climbing into bed.

One falls asleep when
he blinks and bows his head.

2

Two little sleepyheads
breathing soft and low.

One falls asleep
making shadows with his toe.

One little sleepyhead
counting back from ten.

Is he asleep?

Well, here we go again!

Fig. 1 Firefly

Fig. 4 Yellow Beetle with Black Spots

Fig. 2 Southern Green Stink Bug

Fig. 3 Red and Black Beetle

Fig. 5 Winged Desert Termite

Fig. 6 Bumblebee

Fig. 9 Sweet Potato Weevil

Fig. 7 Bush Katydid

Fig. 8 Slug Moth Caterpillar

Fig. 10 Woolly Caterpillar

Enjoy more great picture books from Bloomsbury Children's Books ...

Where is Coco Going?
Sloane Tanen

Clementine and Mungo
Sarah Dyer

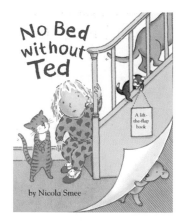

No Bed Without Ted
Nicola Smee

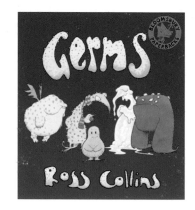

Germs
Ross Collins